Children It's Time to Meet Your Teeth

AMANDA JONES R. N.

amazel
ENTERPRISE

ISBN-13: 978-1544989259
ISBN-10: 1544989253

INTRODUCTION

Want your children to know all about their teeth? Then get this book NOW!!!

This book gives children a better understanding of their teeth, why and how to take care of it. Just like nursery rhymes, children get the bonus of learning in a rhyming format.

Studies have demonstrated that the better children are at detecting rhymes the quicker and more successful they will be at learning to read (Bradley, 1988c, Bradley & Bryant, 1983, Ellis & Large, 1987).

The rhymes in 'Children It's Time To Meet Your Teeth' help to educate and encourage children to explore and establish a proper oral hygiene routine early in life. This helps to ensure the development of strong and healthy teeth, a key feature shown in their beautiful smile.

Book Cover & Layout Engineer: Arbëresh Dalipi
Illustration: Julia Gnedia
Publisher: Amazel Enterprise
Creative Consultant: Engel Jones

CHAPTER 1

MEET YOUR TEETH

Hello, My name is Incisor also called your "front middle teeth". There are other canines and molars which you will later meet.

I usually appear first, around 6-10 months of age,
Then the others come out to give your mouth full coverage.

If you are wondering just how many?
I'll tell you, in total, there are twenty.

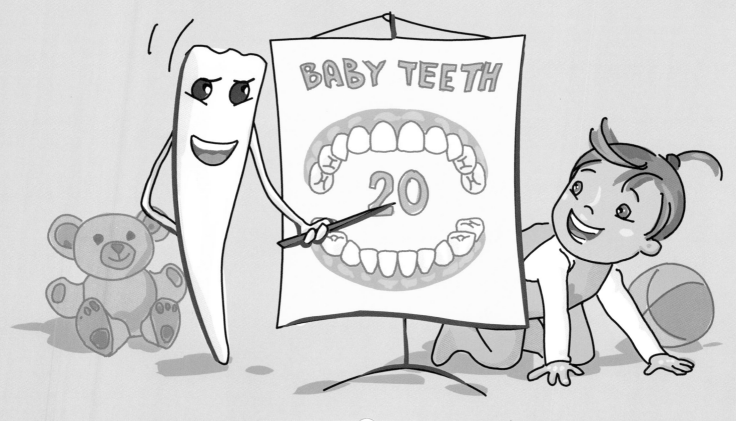

As baby teeth we first start, then later fall out,
To make room for the permanent teeth within your mouth.

Around age six that's when this change is due,
And when it's complete in total, you should have thirty-two.

CHAPTER 2

WHAT DO WE DO?

Each tooth has an important duty
But altogether, we show when you are happy.

When you wear that smile, we are highlighted,
So taking care of us should get you excited.

We also help you to form your words properly,
So when you speak, you do so quite clearly.

We also have the important role,
Of biting and chewing food to be swallowed.

Without us your smile may not be as bright,
Your words may not sound right and your food
you may not be able to bite.

THANK YOU!

CHAPTER 3

DIFFERENT SHAPE,
DIFFERENT JOB

We have different shapes and different names,
To do different jobs which give us our fame.

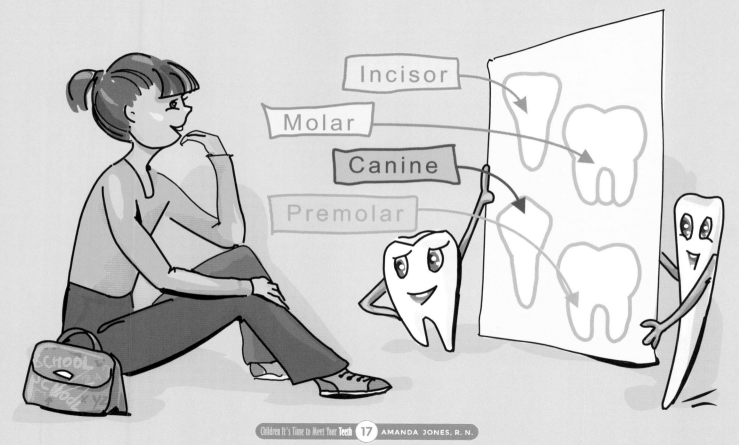

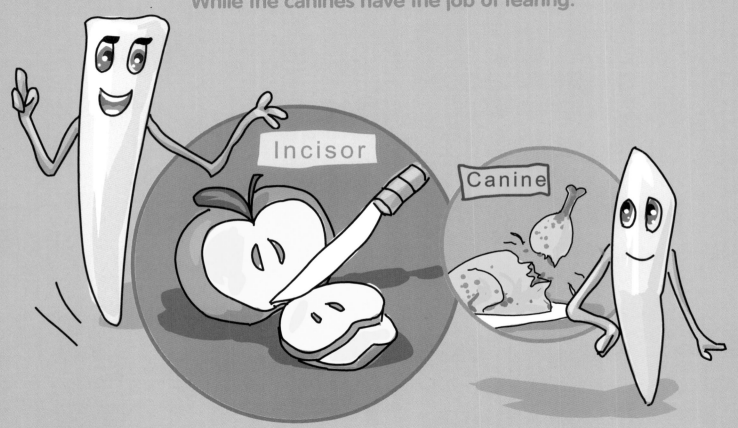

Incisors like me are for cutting,
While the canines have the job of tearing.

Molars and pre-molars grind up your food,
Small enough to swallow after it has been chewed.

Premolar

Molar

Here I will show you pictures of us,
So that you and your friends can discuss.

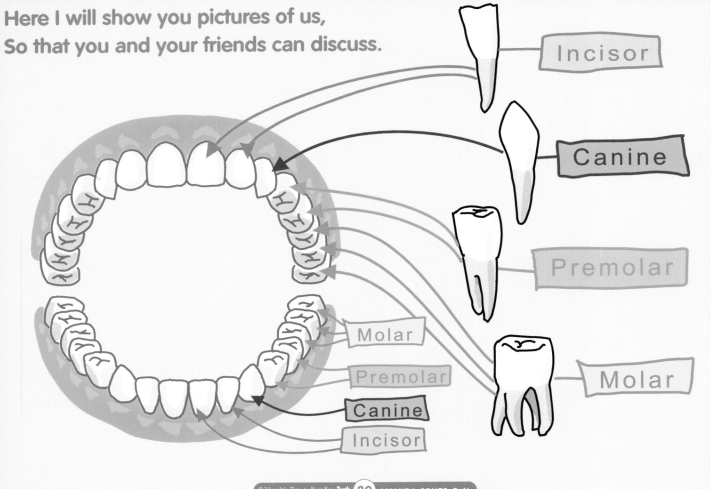

Incisor

Canine

Premolar

Molar

Molar

Premolar

Canine

Incisor

CHAPTER 4
DIFFERENT PARTS OF YOUR TOOTH

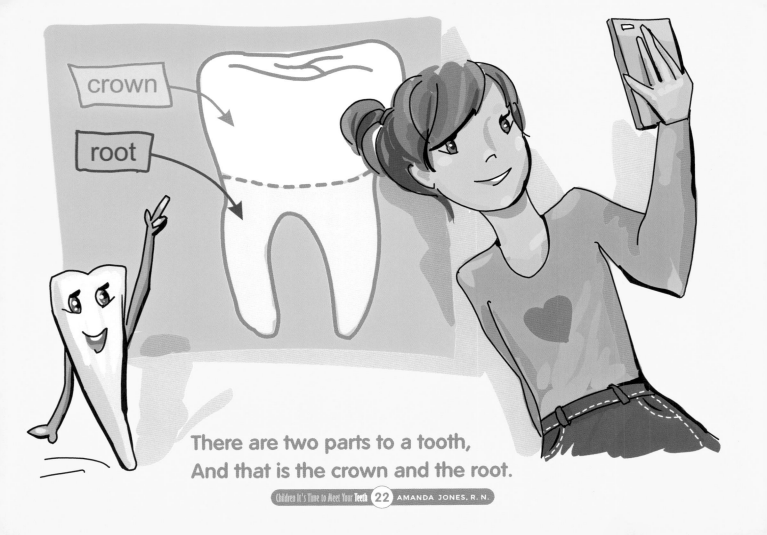

crown

root

There are two parts to a tooth,
And that is the crown and the root.

Inside of your mouth you can see our crown,
While our root is in your jaw bone, all the way down.

The root holds us all steady,
So we can do our job properly.

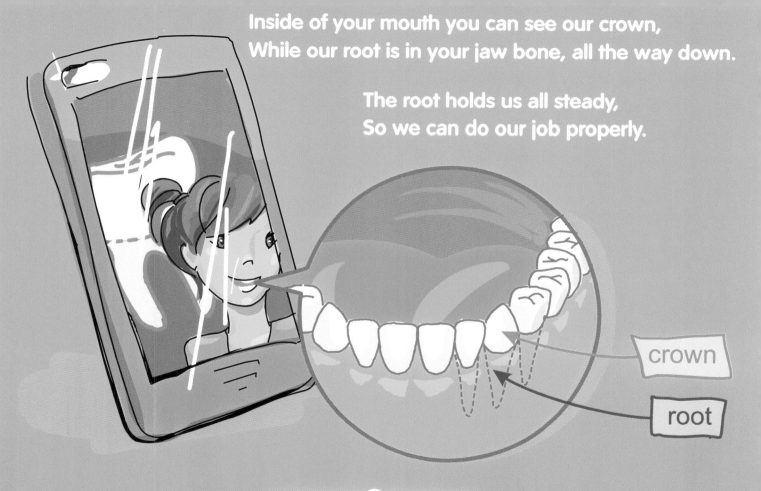

crown

root

Each tooth has three layers, which you should learn really well.
The first is a hard, protective outer layer called the "ENAMEL".

Covering our nerve is another protective layer called the dentin.
Then there is the pulp which has blood
vessels and nerve endings.

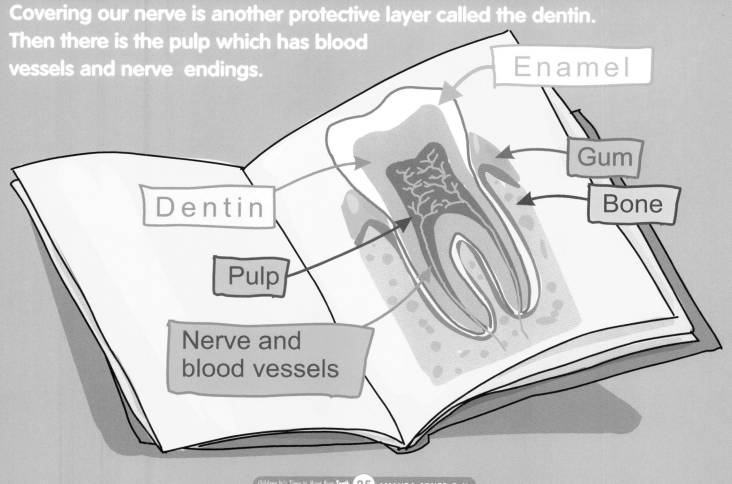

Enamel

Dentin

Gum

Bone

Pulp

Nerve and
blood vessels

CHAPTER 5
WHAT CAN HAPPEN TO US?

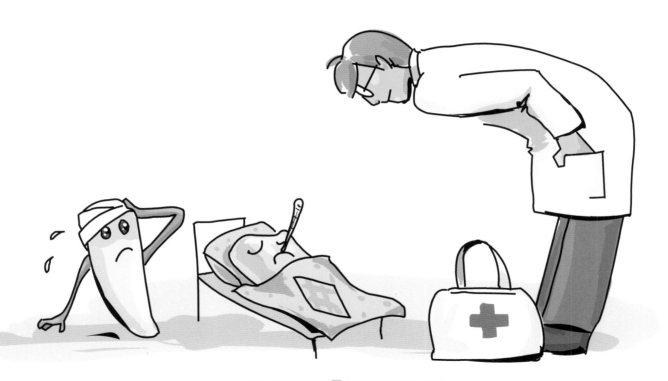

Inside of your mouth is where we will stay,
But germs in your mouth can grow on us everyday.

Germs

Enamel

When you do not take care of us,
These germs can make us fuss.

The germs build up to become dental plaque,
And our outer layers, they begin to attack.

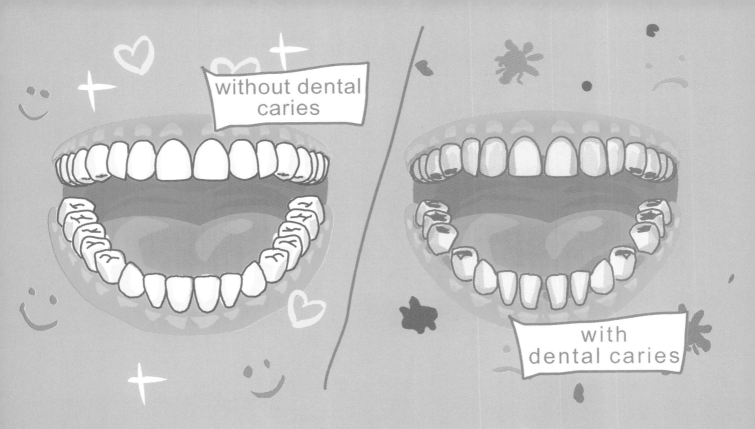

Our protection is weakened and rotted away,
Which result in dental caries or tooth decay.

In its early stages with us you will feel okay,
But it can get worse if you don't take care of us every single day.

CHAPTER 6
HABITS FOR A BRIGHTER SMILE

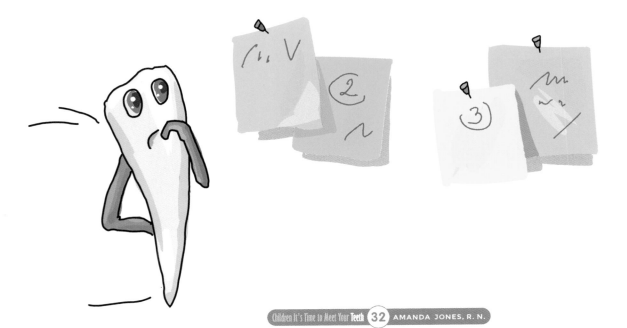

Habits are things you do often,
So practice good hygiene habits if you want to win.

If not, cavities, tooth ache, bleeding gums,
yellow teeth and bad breath,
Are just some of the things which you can get.

To avoid these from happening to you,
There are some hygiene rules which you should stick to.

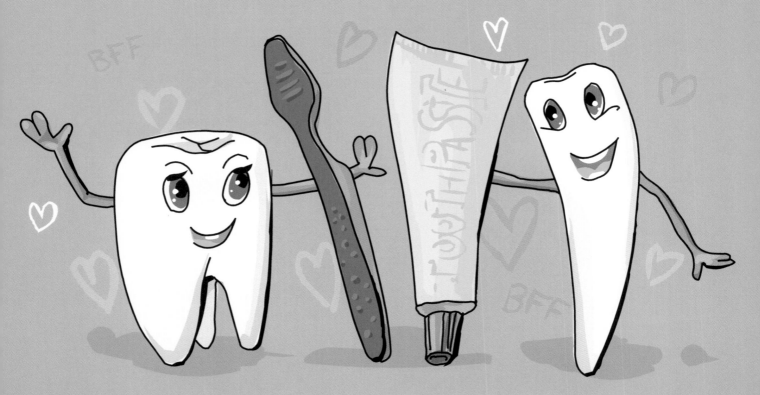

A tooth brush and tooth paste are important tools,
When carrying out the dental hygiene rules.

A small toothbrush with soft bristles should be used,
As large, hard or medium bristles can leave your gums bruised.

Children It's Time to Meet Your Teeth 37 AMANDA JONES, R. N.

Every day, at least twice a day your teeth should be brushed,
And to clean between your teeth,
you should use dental floss.

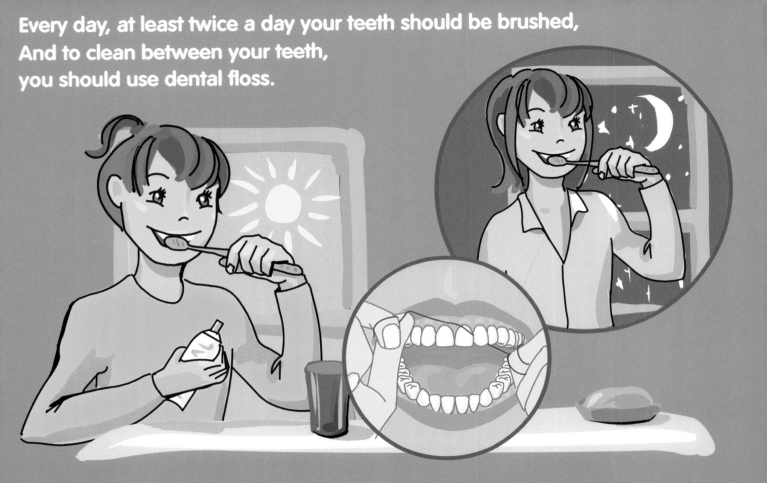

A variety of healthy foods are best for your teeth,
As your body is affected by the type of food which you eat.

At the dentist office your teeth will be checked,
To ensure your hygiene rules were
correct.

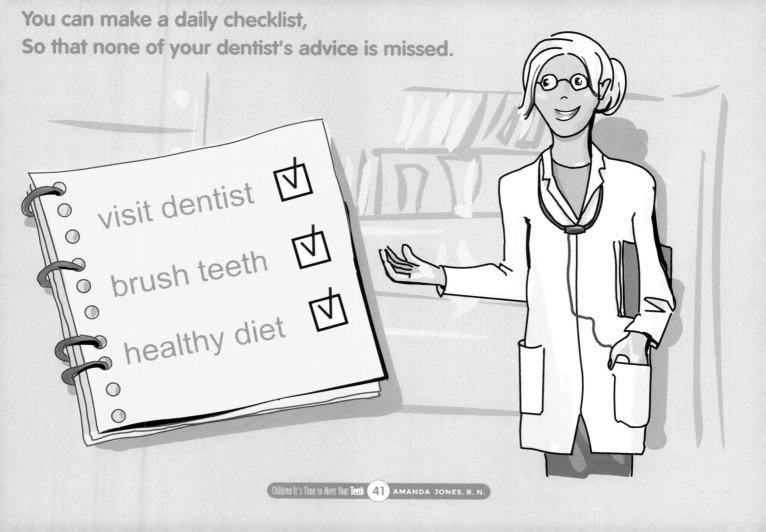

You can make a daily checklist,
So that none of your dentist's advice is missed.

visit dentist ☑
brush teeth ☑
healthy diet ☑

Once you make the hygiene rules an everyday lifestyle,
So much brighter will be your BEAUTIFUL SMILE.

CROSSWORD

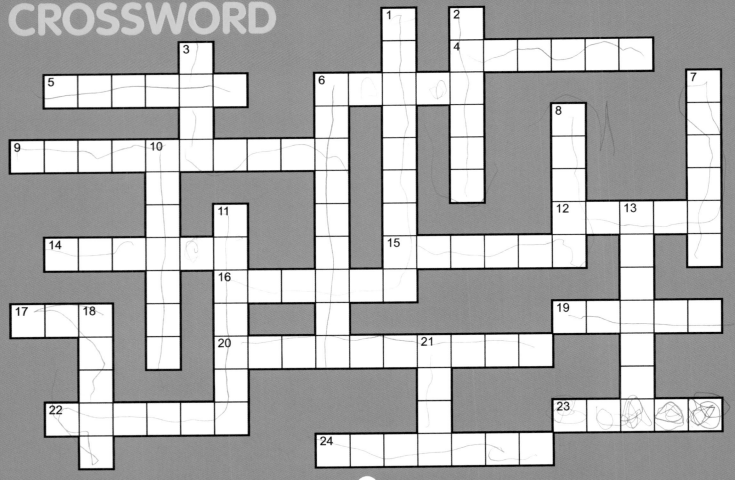

Across

4. the part of a tooth that is attached to the gum

5. a thin coating that forms on teeth and contains bacteria

6. the part of a tooth that can be seen

9. a hole formed in a tooth by decay

12. a hole formed in a tooth by decay

14. a pointed tooth used for tearing

15. a thin coating that forms on teeth and contains bacteria

16. an idea or opinion offered as help in making a choice or a decision.

17. the flesh inside the mouth around the base of the teeth.

19. occurring, made, or acted upon every day

20. a hole formed in a tooth by decay

22. a hole formed in a tooth by decay

23. a hole formed in a tooth by decay

24. a doctor who specializes in teeth, gums, and the mouth.

Down

1. a hole formed in a tooth by decay

2. a thin coating that forms on teeth and contains bacteria

3. a thin coating that forms on teeth and contains bacteria

6. a list of things to be checked or done

7. a thin coating that forms on teeth and contains bacteria

8. waxed or unwaxed thread used to remove food particles and plaque from between the teeth and under the gums.

10. a thin coating that forms on teeth and contains bacteria

11. being free from sickness

13. a tooth that has a sharp edge for cutting

18. the part of a tooth that is attached to the gum

21. the part of a tooth that is attached to the gum

ADVICE, BITE, BLOOD, BREATH, BRISTLES, CANINE, CARIES, CAVITY, CHECKLIST, CHEW, CROWN, DAILY, DENTIN, DENTIST, ENAMEL, FLOSS, GERMS, GUM, HABITS, HEALTHY, HYGIENE, INCISOR, LAYER, LIFESTYLE, MOLAR, MOUTH, NERVE, PLAQUE, PREMOLAR, PROTECTIVE, PULP, ROOT, SMILE, SWALLOW, TEETH, TOOLS, TOOTHACHE, TOOTHBRUSH, TOOTHPASTE, VESSELS, WIN.

```
K H I K X E B Q D N X X V Q V F C K L S D T F S C
Y E U R H C E R E S M P E Y Q Q H T E C H X J K D
P T N O E N F C N T T O O T H A C H E S Y F U Z U
J H F S E Y S H T U O M L B R S Q G U E R V E S H
F E T I U L P E I K O E U A S E I R A C T F S E F
N Y G C C Y Z C N G T V J L R J B G O H P H A L U
C Y T N L L R K H I H I C K N H V R Q O C L E W Y
H H R I Q E S L G T P T H F T H A D K V T M O L C
E A A E V E C I V D A C O O L L O Z E H A L X E Z
W D B W Y A I S T G S E O O O O A M Y N L X G H E
Q E N I N A C T I N T T R M L Y S F E A T F P G O
O I W N T P L A Q U E O E B Y S R S W L E I J X Q
I I O P H S U T G T B R I S T L E S M R E G S E C
A O R V D U S L I V P P V E S S E L S G V Y U T D
B I C Y S Q F B P U L I F E S T Y L E L I M S M F
```

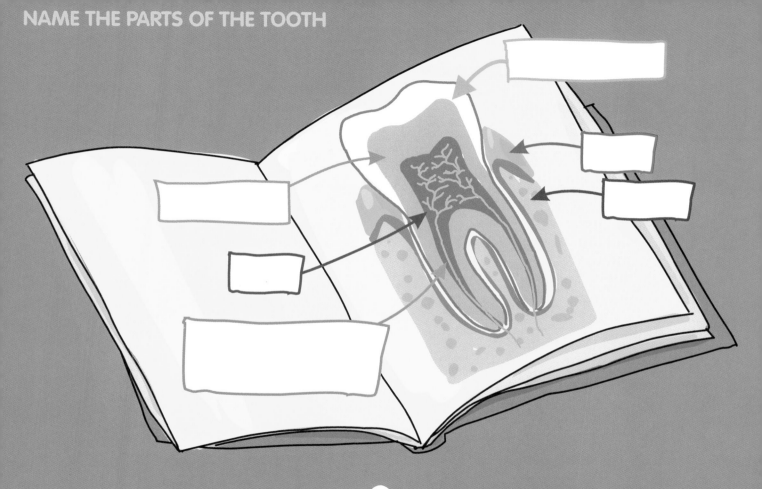

CONTACT:

aj@poemsbyaj.com

www.poemsbyaj.com

/NurseJonesChat

/amandajohnjones

Amanda Jones

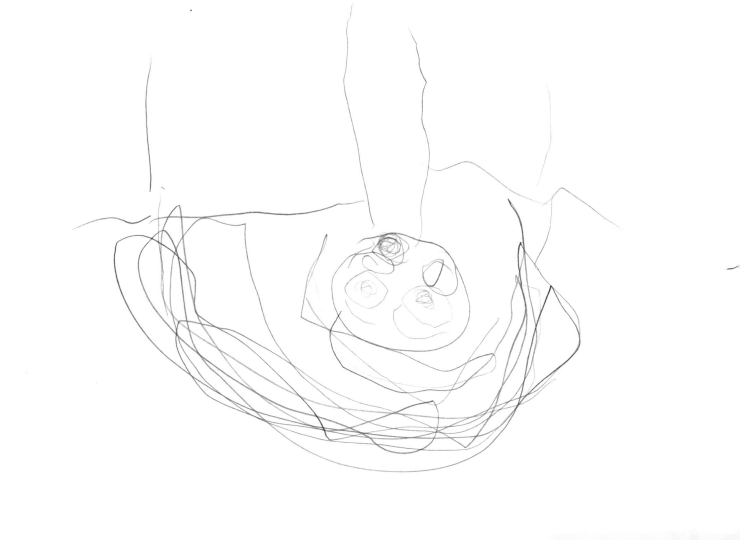

Printed in Great Britain
by Amazon